THE GOLDEN YEARS

1961

text: David Sandison, Arthur Davis

design: Paul Kurzeja

SIENA

196

Welcome to *The Golden Years* and your chance to remember and relive the people and events which made 1961 a truly remarkable year. It was a year which saw John Kennedy take his place as the youngest-ever President of the United States, signalling his dreams of a new age by asking US citizens to join his revolution. It was a year which saw the Soviet Union win the first stage of the space race with the US by putting Yuri Gagarin into orbit. It was a year in which Britain yielded to the 'wind of change' which Prime Minister Harold Macmillan had said was sweeping through Africa, and released Kenyan freedom fighter Jomo Kenyatta from eight years of pointless imprisonment.

East Germany took the world by surprise when it sealed its West Berlin boundary with a wall which would symbolize the gulf between communism and capitalism. Rudolph Nureyev would leap that gulf and seek the freedom to dance wherever he wanted. United Nations chief Däg Hammarskjöld would pay the ultimate price - his own life - trying to bridge the gulf between warring factions in the newly independent Congo.

Israel finally had the chance to punish a monster by capturing Adolf Eichmann, a man who perfected a system for the greatest atrocity in history, and

Cubans exiled in the US failed to punish Fidel Castro, the man they believed had stolen their homeland, when the Bay of Pigs invasion turned into a fiasco. While we mourned the loss of Gary Cooper, Sir Thomas Beecham, Carl Jung and Ernest Hemingway, Tottenham Hotspur celebrated their supremacy in English football by becoming the first team this century to win the League and FA Cup double. Sharks and Jets rumbled in West Side Story, the New York folk scene buzzed with the arrival of a young Bob Dylan and, in Liverpool, a man called Brian Epstein decided to manage a group called The Beatles.

It's all here, and a lot more besides!

Kennedy Takes Oath As Youngest President

THE OLDEST US President in history today handed over the duty of running the United States of America to the youngest man ever elected to the post when Dwight D Eisenhower, the 70-year-old retiring Republican President, was the first to shake the hand of 43-year-old John F Kennedy, after the charismatic Democrat was sworn in as the 35th President in Washington.

Kennedy's first speech as President stressed his desire for peace, which he hoped the USSR shared, and to whom he suggested exploratory discussions on the future of nuclear weapons and eventual disarmament, while making it clear that the US would fight against any threatening force.

The most quoted passage of his speech came when he memorably challenged the American people: 'Ask not what your country can do for you - ask what you can do for your country.' Kennedy emphasized his belief in traditional values becoming part of a new youthful initiative, when he attended his inauguration wearing full dress suit, including a top hat.

The new President also proved that 'the torch has been passed to a new generation of Americans' by making his Inauguration Ball that night a romping knees-up. Dispensing with the usual staid fare of palm court orchestras, he and his guests were entertained by a swinging Frank Sinatra.

Old Blue Eyes Launches Own Record Label

Reprise Records was the name chosen by the internationally popular vocal star, Frank Sinatra, for the new record label he launched in Los Angeles this month, and on which his future recordings would be released.

After gaining fame singing with the orchestras of Harry James and Tommy Dorsey in the 1940s, Sinatra embarked on a highly successful solo career with Capitol Records. Following acclaimed albums like *Songs For Swinging Lovers* and numerous hit singles, Sinatra decided to launch Reprise, presumably to allow him greater artistic freedom and a bigger share of the proceeds.

There was speculation about which other artists would join him, and among the names mentioned were Dean Martin and Sammy Davis Jr, both Sinatra's close friends and members of his so-called 'rat pack'.

JANUARY 31

US Space Chimp Returns Safely

With NASA's new *Mercury* space capsule almost ready to tranport a human pilot into the stratosphere and beyond, the 18 minute voyage of a chimpanzee named Ham - who was flown 150 miles above the earth today, and returned to earth with a smile on his face and apparently unharmed - was a necessary exercise.
Not only did Ham survive, but NASA's chosen method of returning and retrieving its future space capsules from the ocean rather than the Soviet Union's more risky touchdowns on land, was obviously effective.

UK TOP 10 SINGLES

1: Poetry In Motion
- Johnny Tillotson
2: I Love You
- Cliff Richard
3: Save The Last Dance For Me
- The Drifters
4: Portrait Of My Love
- Matt Monro
5: It's Now Or Never
- Elvis Presley
6: Perfidia
- The Ventures
7: Counting Teardrops
- Emile Ford & The Checkmates
8: Are You Lonesome Tonight
- Elvis Presley
9: Goodness Gracious Me
- Peter Sellers and Sophia Loren
10: Buona Sera
- Acker Bilk

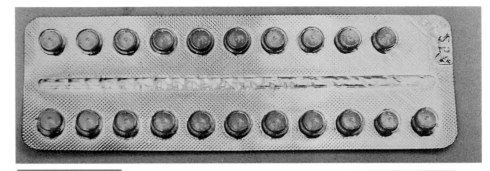

JANUARY 30

Contraceptive Pill Shifts Birth Control Onus

The introduction today of Conovid, a pill which women can take to avoid becoming pregnant, ushered in a new era for sexual politics in Britain. The traditional birth control method, male condoms, appeared to be under attack as women gained control over the process for the first time.

The idea was for women to swallow a small contraceptive pill on prescribed days during their menstrual cycles; this was supposed to guarantee that pregnancy would not occur, and relieve males of the burden of responsibility for safe sex. Extensive tests were carried out before the pill became available, firstly to ensure that it produced the desired result and, equally importantly, to learn of potentially dangerous side-effects. These were known to include nausea, headaches, weight gain, breast engorgement and pre-menstrual tension, but all were said to vanish after a few months.

JANUARY 8

De Gaulle Wins National 'Oui' For Algerian Line

More than 15 million French and Algerian voters gave an unconditional 'Oui' to President Charles de Gaulle's policy of home rule for Algeria today when over 75 per cent of those entitled to vote also signalled their hope that he could start to resolve the long and bloody Algerian conflict via talks.

There was concern that five million people - too large a minority to ignore - voted 'Non' to indicate their continued resistance to France releasing Algeria. The General knew that while he'd won an important battle, the war itself still remained to be won.

Spy Scare As Five Arrested In London

BRITAIN WAS GRIPPED by spy fever today following the arrest of five people by Special Branch officers on suspicion of espionage. Three Canadians and two English civil servants were accused of conspiring to pass on secret documents relating to naval defence research kept at the Royal Navy's Underwater Warfare headquarters in the quiet county of Dorset in south-west England.

Civil servants Harold Houghton and Ethel Gee were arrested at London's Waterloo Station after being watched handing a package to Canadian businessman Gordon Lonsdale. Also held were Peter and Helen Kroger, two other Canadians living in outer London.

Scotland Yard sources intimated that some of those arrested may in fact be Russians. All five were held in custody while searches were made of a house occupied by the Krogers, described by neighbours as 'a very nice, ordinary couple'.

Belgians Fly Troops In To Rescue Congo Whites

Belgian paratroops were reported en route to the Congo town of Stanleyville today, with a mission to rescue more than 1,000 Europeans trapped in a reign of terror by supporters of Patrice Lumumba, the West African nation's deposed Prime Minister.

Crowds of drunken troops were reported to be rampaging through Stanleyville, beating Belgian men and raping their wives. The attacks were said to be reprisals for the recent arrest of Lumumba, and the Congo government's decision to hand him over to the pro-Western Katanga region leader, Moise Tshombe.

Feline Film Star Purrs No More

Elsa, probably the most famous lioness of all time as the star of the hit movie *Born Free*, died today on the Masai Mara reserve, in Kenya.

Born Free, which starred Bill Travers and Virginia McKenna, was based on the book by British naturalist Joy Adamson, which related the true story of her life dedicated to saving African wild-life. She had nursed Elsa from a cub.

FEB

Lumumba Dies While 'Escaping' Congo Captors

PATRICE LUMUMBA, (pictured) the fiery first Prime Minister of the newly independent West African state of Congo, was reported dead today, allegedly killed by villagers in a remote bush region of Katanga.

According to an announcement made by Katanga's Minister of the Interior, Godefroid Munongo, in Elisabethville, Lumumba and two colleagues had been killed after escaping from custody on January 17. The former premier had been sent to Katanga pending his trial on charges of inciting the Congolese army to mutiny and had already escaped prison in December. The Minister showed journalists death certificates, which simply certified that Lumumba and his supporters had died, but omitted stating the cause of death.

The villagers who found and executed Lumumba had been paid a bounty of £3,000 ($9,000), Mr Munongo confirmed, making it plain that he was pleased to see the back of a man he described as 'an ordinary criminal reponsible for thousands of deaths'.

News of Lumumba's death - and the fact that a European pilot who flew him to Katanga reported that police had beaten Lumumba severely during the flight - fuelled international outrage. On February 19, London police battled with protestors who staged a march on the Belgian Embassy.

1: Are You Lonesome Tonight
- Elvis Presley
2: Sailor
- Petula Clark
3: Rubber Ball
- Bobby Vee
4: You're Sixteen
- Johnny Burnette
5: Pepe
- Duane Eddy
6: Portrait Of My Love
- Matt Monro
7: FBI
- The Shadows
8: Poetry In Motion
- Johnny Tillotson
9: Walk Right Back
- The Everly Brothers
10: Sailor
- Anne Shelton

FEBRUARY 25

Kennedy Appoints Academic To Major Government Post

Remaining true to his election pledge to inject new blood into his government by recruiting key advisers from leading American universities, US President John Kennedy today appointed Dr Henry Kissinger to a position of considerable importance in the new team which will run the United States.

A noted academic, the German born Kissinger's particular responsibility will be in the field of national security. Educated at Harvard, the 48 year-old was appointed Professor of Government there in 1958, a post he will retain.

FEBRUARY 21

Rhodesian Leader Rejects Increased Black Power

Just four days after abandoning London talks relating to a new constitution, Sir Roy Welensky, Northern Rhodesia's Prime Minister, caused fresh controversy today when he refused to countenance a British proposal for increased black participation in his country's legislature.

Perhaps anticipating that anti-apartheid demonstrators might cause trouble as a result of his rejection of Britain's latest power-sharing suggestion, he also ordered the call-up of 3,000 Territorial troops 'to deal with any insurrection'. Sir Roy had made clear his basic disagreement with the British government's desire to further the cause of equality. His view was that if Africans were given too much influence too quickly, there was a risk of what he called 'debasing the franchise' if power slipped from 'responsible' (white) hands.

FEBRUARY 20

The Final Frontier Falls Again

Space may be, in the timeless words of *Star Trek*, 'the final frontier', but earth's scientists managed to make light of it again this month with two spectacular examples of ingenuity and technological brilliance.

On February 12, Soviet space authorities confirmed that they had successfully launched what they described as an 'interplanetary space station'. Given that they had not yet managed to put a man into space, their ambition was commendable - the station was aimed at the planet Venus.

Scientists at Britain's Jodrell Bank had already 'bounced' radio signals off the moon to contact fellow boffins in the US. On February 24 they went one better, disregarding the quarter of a million miles or so of nothingness between us and our only natural satellite, they managed to transmit telegraph signals to Australia!

FEBRUARY 24

Leakey And Lucy Re-Write Mankind's History

New fossil bones unearthed by British anthropologist Dr Louis Leakey in Tanganyika were said today to push the origins of human-like species back to around one million years ago - almost twice as old as his previous finds. Like those, the new Leakey fossils - a skull, a collarbone, part of the hands and a foot of a child thought to have been about 11 years old - were found by Dr Leakey (pictured) in the remote Olduvai Gorge. He decided to name the skull 'Lucy', bringing her to London for more extensive and detailed tests. One thing he was pretty sure about: Lucy had probably been murdered. A crack in the skull was consistent with a heavy blow.

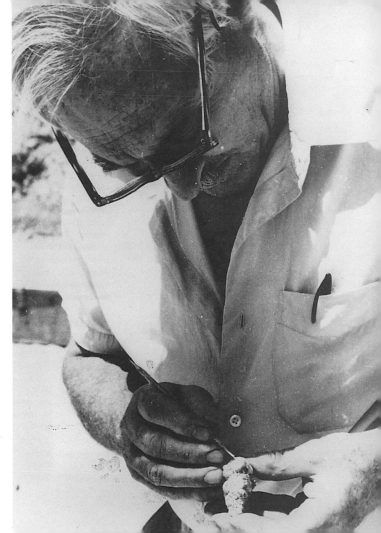

BBC Chiefs Axe Children's Hour After 39 Years

BBC RADIO bosses proved that the times really were a'changing today when they confirmed that the long running daily *Children's Hour* programme would be discontinued in April. Audiences for the much-admired programme, which first began in 1922, had substantially decreased in the face of competition from television, with no more than 250,000 listeners remaining faithful to the somewhat parental intonations of the programme's host, veteran children's broadcaster Derek McCulloch, known universally as 'Uncle Mac'.

In the world of *Oh Boy!* and other teenage-oriented television shows, *Children's Hour* had become an anachronism - though many would mourn that Anthony Buckridge's adventures of schoolboys Jennings, Darbishire and their teachers (Retsim Retrac had always been a favourite), and series like *Malcolm Saville's Gay Dolphin Adventure* would no longer entrance children with the wonder of radio drama.

Only time would tell whether British youngsters would take to a new programme rather patronisingly titled *Playtime,* or a Saturday morning record request show, *Children's Favourites,* which seemed certain to attract teenagers rather than their younger siblings.

Black Teen-Idol Jackie Shot

Jackie Wilson, the 27-year-old performer who'd become to black teenagers in the 1960s what Elvis Presley was to white kids in the 1950s, was rushed to hospital in New York tonight after being shot by a female fan he'd tried to persuade not to commit suicide.

The incident happened at Wilson's apartment when the fan, named as 28-year-old Juanita Jones, became hysterical and threatened to shoot herself. Doctors decided not to remove the bullet, which was lodged dangerously near vital organs, and the singer - who had a remarkable seven records in the *Billboard* charts in 1960 - was able to leave hospital after a few days treatment and rest.

Wilson's career would be cut tragically short in 1975 when he suffered a heart attack and went into a coma from which he never recovered. He finally died in January 1984, unaware that his 1957 hit *Reet Petite* had achieved classic status, becoming a re-issued British No 1 in 1986, while his *Higher And Higher* would also re-emerge as a 1987 hit.

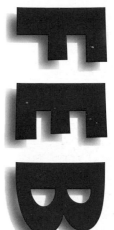

Irish Soccer Star Refuses TV Accolade

Irish international and Tottenham Hotspur soccer star Danny Blanchflower gave TV presenter Eamonn Andrews, host of the top rated *This Is Your Life*, the shock of his life today when he became the first ever show target to refuse the invitation to have his past life flash before him.

Andrews, himself an Irishman, might have expected that Blanchflower would be only too pleased to renew his acquaintance with members of his family, colleagues, and others with whom he may have fallen out of touch. But Blanchflower was unwilling to play this particular game, which he obviously felt was an unwelcome invasion of his privacy!

Benn Barred From Commons

Labour Party rebel Anthony Wedgwood Benn, who became Viscount Stansgate on the death of his father last November, lost the latest round of his fight to stay an ordinary Member of Parliament today when the House of Commons Privileges Committee confirmed his disqualification as an MP.

The young left-winger had tried to resign his peerage last year, but this had been refused by the Queen. As a peer, he could not remain in the Commons, though Stansgate/Benn was determined to explore every loophole. He had already said he intended to run in the Bristol by-election the government had called in May to replace him.

MARCH 8

Beecham, Musical Magician, Dies

Sir Thomas Beecham, the man who used a family fortune to found four great British orchestras and become one of the world's most brilliant conductors, died today, aged 81.

A member of the Beecham's Liver Pills empire, Sir Thomas dedicated himself to music from an early age, using the company's huge profits to create the Royal Philharmonic Orchestra, and the London Philharmonic. A noted patron of new talent, he brought Diaghelev's ballet company and the legendary Nijinsky to Britain.

As a witty and waspish conductor, 'Tommy' (as he was affectionately known to his musicians) championed the works of Mozart, Delius, Strauss and Sibelius and left behind a fine legacy of superb recordings.

Jaguar Unveils The Shape Of The Sixties

Launched this month by Jaguar, the sleek sporty E-Type was an instant hit with motoring journalists and younger drivers with an itch to handle what was destined to become one of the most distinctive style icons of the Swinging Sixties. Capable of reaching 150 mph (247 kph) and cruising at 100 mph, the E-Type set eager buyers back a nifty £2,196 (about $6,300).

South Africa To Break From Common-wealth

INCREASINGLY ISOLATED from the rest of Africa and subject to international condemnation for its racist apartheid regime, South Africa signalled its intention to go it alone today when Prime Minister Hendrick Verwoerd confirmed that the country would cut its ties with the British Commonwealth when it became independent at the end of May.

This was the inevitable result of the growing world pressure for reform - and South Africa's refusal to change. Defending his government's stand, Dr Verwoerd predicted that the Commonwealth would fall apart if each member state were not allowed to decide its own destiny.

He said that withdrawal was to prevent Great Britain and other founder member countries from conflict with the emergent nations, and pointedly noted: 'It is clear that we will no longer be welcome.'

Born this month:

11: Bruce Watson, UK pop musician (Big Country); Mike Percy, UK rock musician (Dead Or Alive)

21: Lothar Matthäus, German international soccer star

27: Clark Datcher, UK pop musician (Johnny Hates Jazz)

DEPARTURES

Died this month:

6: George Formby, British comedian, music hall star *(see main story)*

8: Sir Thomas Beecham, British conductor, orchestra founder *(see main story)*

MARCH 1

Peace Corps Launched By Kennedy

Having told Americans, in his inauguration speech, to ask what they could do for their country, President Kennedy today asked his young citizens to sign up for a Peace Corps which would work 'in the great common cause of world developments.' Volunteers would receive no payment for their work, but young Americans of both sexes would have the chance to work and live with local people, teach in local schools and speak local languages, and no doubt try to spread America's philosophies and way of life in emerging Third World countries. Kennedy explained that for volunteers 'life will not be easy, but it will be rich and satisfying.' The scheme planned to have 1,000 volunteers in place by year end.

MARCH 13

Picasso Weds Model

Pablo Picasso, the controversial Spanish-born artist at the heart of many major new movements during the past 30 years, today married his favourite model, Jacqueline Roque, in Nice. Artists marrying models is nothing new, of course. But Picasso was now aged 79, while his bride was a mere 37 years old.

MARCH 6

George Stops Cleaning Windows

One of Britain's most enduring and popular music hall veterans, comedian, *double entendre* champion and ukelele wizard, George Formby, died today. He was 57 years old.

Formby, born George Hoy Booth, took his name from the Lancashire town in which he was born and raised. He climbed quickly through the ranks of British variety bills to become a major star in the 1930s. While some of his hit records were shunned by the BBC as too rude (*When I'm Cleaning Windows, With My Little Stick Of Blackpool Rock* included), his version of *Leaning On A Lampost* was one of the most-played records of its time.

The coming of television and decline of music halls inevitably meant a drop in Formby's workload and when he failed to translate his talents to the small screen, early retirement was the only real option for the man who once reigned supreme.

US Increases Arms And Aid For Laos

PRESIDENT JOHN F KENNEDY spelled out the United States' determination to help halt continued Communist advances in South-East Asia today in Washington when he told a press conference that an extra 100 US advisers were to be posted to Laos.

The President's package to Laos, where the Pathet Lao communist movement was threatening the Laotian government, would also see the United States providing additional arms and financial assistance to combat the threat posed by guerrillas who were threatening the country's stability.

Using Soviet-supplied arms, the Pathet Lao were mainly targeting outlying rural areas. Bordered by China, Vietnam, Cambodia, Thailand and Burma, Laos was a strategic bulwark against the spread of communism, but President Kennedy's officials were quick to stress that the US was not engaged in an arms race with the USSR.

'WEST SIDE STORY' WINS TEN IN CONFUSING OSCARS NIGHT

The voting members of The Academy of Motion Pictures Arts and Sciences never seem to tire of delivering verdicts which appear to defy any form of logic employed by us lesser mortals - nominating certain films as Best Picture while ignoring their directors and stars (so what makes a picture worth considered 'best'?) - while piling on a long list of nominations for those who made a film worth its Best Picture short-listing, but giving the Oscars to people whose movies weren't even nominated for anything else.

The inclusion of *Fanny* in this year's Best Picture shortlist was a case in point. A slight and silly film by any standard, it was the screen version of a hit Broadway musical - with the songs taken out ! Director Joshua Logan didn't get nominated, neither did two of its three co-stars, Charles Boyer, Maurice Chevalier and Leslie Caron. Boyer found himself in competition with Paul Newman (for *The Hustler*), Spencer Tracy and eventual winner Maximilian Schell (for *Judgment At Nuremberg*) and Stuart Whitman (for the otherwise un-nominated *The Mark*).

The failure of a seven-times nominated *The Hustler* (for Best Picture, Robert Rossen as Director, Newman as Best Actor, Piper Laurie as Best Actress, George C Scott and Jackie Gleason as Best Supporting Actor) to win anything except a Black and White Cinematography Oscar for Eugen Shuftan, will long remain a mystery.

Hit - and multi-Oscar winner - of the year was *West Side Story*. Besides being voted Best Picture and giving co-directors Robert Wise and Jerome Robbins the unique achievement of being the only two-man directorial team ever to win the prized statuette, it gave George Chakiris and Rita Moreno well-deserved Supporting Actor and Actress awards, and trophies for its cinematographer, its score, art direction, costume design and sound - ten prizes in all.

Missing out on a Best Actress nomination for *West Side Story*, Natalie Wood did make it for *Splendor In The Grass*, but lost out to Sophia Loren who, with the Italian language *Two Women*, became the only person ever to win an Oscar for a film not in English.

While there were many who thought Audrey Hepburn's performance in the quirky *Breakfast At Tiffany's* ought to have won her a Best Actress award, few argued with the decision to give Henry Mancini and Johnny Mercer Oscars for the movie's timeless theme song, *Moon River*.

The multi-Oscar winning
'West Side Story'

APRIL

Cliff Starts Work On First Major Movie

Obviously determined to emulate the big screen success of his long-time hero, Elvis Presley, British rock star Cliff Richard began work on his first starring role this month. The film - a musical - was to be titled *The Young Ones*. Although Cliff had appeared in two previous films, *Serious Charge* and *Expresso Bongo,* both had been 'straight' dramatic roles which thrilled only his most fanatical fans. The decision to give him a chance to do what he did best - sing and dance - would prove a wise one when *The Young Ones* was released in January 1962. Heavyweight acting would come from Robert Morley, playing Cliff's businessman father, while the love interest would be supplied by Carole Gray.

APRIL 16

Country Music Goes Big-Time

Country music received the biggest boost to its credibility in Jacksonville, Florida, today when the first official Country Music Festival was staged by the recently formed Country Music Association.
Staged at the Jacksonville Coliseum, the all-star line-up included Patsy Cline, Webb Pierce, Faron Young, George Hamilton IV, Lester Flatt and Earl Scruggs, The Louvin Brothers, Porter Wagoner and Mel Tillis.

USSR Wins Race To Put Man In Space

THE SOVIET UNION put itself firmly into the lead in the space race again today when Russian cosmonaut Major Yuri Gagarin (pictured) became the first human being to experience space travel. Gagarin's flight of over 100 minutes in a Vostok spaceship, at a height of 190 miles, took in a complete circuit of the earth before he returned unharmed to *terra firma*.

There had been speculation in Moscow that this momentous event was about to take place because it had been an open secret that the Soviet Space Agency had such an expedition planned for some time. As confirmation of Gagarin's flight was broadcast by Radio Moscow, thousands of Russians flooded on to the streets to celebrate.

Soviet premier Nikita Khrushchev was one of the first to commend the 27-year-old Gagarin's achievement, and the two men spoke on the telephone soon after the cosmonaut disembarked from his craft. Gagarin reported that he felt well. 'I have no injuries or bruises,' he reassured Khrushchev.

Even Russia's rivals in the space race were fulsome in their praise. James Webb, head of the American space agency, NASA, called Gagarin's exploit: 'a fantastic, fabulous achievement.'

UK TOP 10 SINGLES

1: Wooden Heart
- Elvis Presley
2: Are You Sure
- The Allisons
3: Lazy River
- Bobby Darin
4: You're Driving Me Crazy
- The Temperance Seven
5: Exodus
- Ferrante & Teicher
6: Theme For A Dream
- Cliff Richard
7: Where The Boys Are
- Connie Francis
8: Blue Moon
- The Marcels
9: Walk Right Back
- The Everly Brothers
10: And The Heavens Cried
- Anthony Newley

APRIL 19

Cuban Exiles Invade Bay Of Pigs

THE STRUGGLE for control of the Caribbean island of Cuba gained momentum this month as the Cuban Revolutionary Council, an armed group of exiles based in Florida, fought a series of battles with the Cuban army (pictured with a captured launch from US employed mercenaries) of the Marxist revolutionary President Fidel Castro.

On April 19, the anti-government forces claimed to have established a runway for aircraft near the Bay Of Pigs, and to be within 70 miles of the Cuban capital, Havana. This was refuted by Castro's commanders who said it was their superior forces, equipped with Russian built tanks and fighter planes, which had won the day. Cuban radio reported that nearly 30 insurgents had been arrested, with eight of them executed.

The turmoil resulted in the two major international powers making threats of greater involvement. On April 20, Soviet leader Nikita Khrushchev accused the exiles of attempting to disrupt Cuba's political *status quo*, and asked the US to 'put an end to the aggression against the Republic of Cuba.'

Promising to provide Russian support for Cuba, Khrushchev referred to the situation in Laos, which also featured Russia and the US on opposing sides. President Kennedy's response was straightforward and blunt - Khrushchev had got it wrong, and the United States would only intervene in Cuba if Russia became involved. This new East-West standoff did little to reassure the rest of the world that peace was any nearer.

APRIL 20

Angolan Nationalists Massacre Whites

As many as 500 whites were reported to have been killed in Portugal's West African colony of Angola in figures released today. They were victims of increased violence resulting from Angolan nationalists' bid to gain independence.

Describing the violence as 'far more terrible than anything that happened in the Belgian Congo', a Portuguese official said his country was involved in 'a life or death struggle' to retain African territory it considered vital to its future.

APRIL 3

Nuclear Protesters Arrested In London Demo

The US Embassy in London's Mayfair was the target for a major protest organized by anti-nuclear campaigners in Grosvenor Square, today.

More than 30 protestors were arrested by police before peace was restored and the demonstration - the biggest staged in the capital for some time - came to an end.

APRIL 21

Nazi Eichmann Admits Murdering Jews

Charged on 15 counts of conspiring to bring about the deaths of millions of Jews as chief administrator of the Nazis' so-called 'final solution' - charges which inevitably carry the death penalty - former SS commander Adolf Eichmann admitted to a Jerusalem court today that he had been involved in 'liquidating' those which Adolf Hitler considered enemies of the state.

Appearing in court inside a cage of bullet proof glass, Eichmann claimed that he was merely responsible for organizing transportation of Jewish prisoners to places of execution. His role in the mass extermination plan had merely been to make its organization more efficient.

'Not every person I evacuated was put to death', Eichmann protested, with warped logic. 'Otherwise, 2,400,000 people would not have been found after the war.'

APRIL 24

De Gaulle Under Siege

Faced with the threat of an armed air invasion by rebel French soldiers from Algeria, President Charles de Gaulle today ordered the fortification of the Elysee Palace, his official residence in Paris, to be surrounded by tanks, with a makeshift force assembled to guard against attack by paratroopers intent on starting a civil war.

Following the capture of Algiers by rebel forces, both Paris civil airports were effectively blockaded by vehicles to prevent attackers landing, and orders were issued for any 'unfriendly' aircraft to be shot down. A sea blockade of Algeria was also enforced, with all commercial activity frozen.

However, later reports suggested that the attempted Algerian coup had failed, and the high-ranking ringleaders, led by General Challe, had all been arrested and stripped of their ranks. While the situation remained tense and uncertain, the President gained some comfort from the fact that the French population was seemingly supporting him.

MAY

Spurs Do The Double!

FOOTBALL HISTORY was made at London's Wembley Stadium today when Tottenham Hotspur, for many years one of England's most popular and high profile football teams, achieved the remarkable feat of winning the two major trophies in English soccer in the same season, the first to do so this century.

Defeating Leicester City in today's FA Cup Final set the seal on a campaign in which Spurs (as the North London team are better known) also collected the First Division Championship.

Maybe Irishman Danny Blanchflower, the Tottenham captain, refused the recent accolade of being the subject of TV's *This Is Your Life* to ensure he was not distracted from his team's main target.

That was not achieved until the final quarter of the Cup Final, when England centre forward Bobby Smith was able to find the net so brilliantly protected up to that point by Gordon Banks, the young Leicester goalkeeper. Nine minutes later, Spurs' Terry Dyson made the trophy secure - and the unique double complete - with a headed goal.

Racists Attack White Liberals In Alabama

A week after fighting broke out in Birmingham, Alabama, between white supremacists intent on retaining their traditional status and so-called 'freedom riders' equally bent on furthering the cause of racial integration, violence spread to another Alabama city, Montgomery, today when segregation laws were flaunted by black and white civil rights workers who refused to sit in bus seats designated as only available to blacks.

Inevitably exciting members of the Ku Klux Klan and others with similar views who'd assembled in Montgomery to preserve segregation, an attack on a busload of 'freedom riders' they felt were flaunting regulations, caused numerous casualties.

The situation became so volatile that a state of martial law was declared by the Governor of Alabama, John Patterson, and Federal marshals were called to provide security at a meeting addressed by the Rev Martin Luther King, where hundreds of white activists surrounded the church, hurling obscene and racist insults.

Mandela Evades SA Round-Ups

Nelson Mandela, the black South African nationalist leader, was tonight reported to have still eluded police teams who arrested most of those who organized today's banned nationwide strike.

Mandela was not at his home in Orlando, near Johannesburg, when police arrived to take him into custody. They were met by his wife, Winnie, who demanded to see a valid search warrant. Officers had to return to a local police HQ for the document. Despite a thorough search of the house and Mandela's papers, they left empty handed.

Today's clamp-down and arrests brought the total of people detained to almost 10,000. Most are believed to be blacks and members of the banned African National Congress. No whites had been arrested, but a number of Asians were said to have been detained. It all boded ill for the future of South Africa, which became a republic on May 31.

MAY 13

Hollywood Mourns Cooper, The Ultimate Cowboy

Hollywood - and everyone who had ever sat nervously on the edge of a cinema seat as he faced down another gang of desperadoes - was saddened today by the death, at the age of 60, of actor Gary Cooper, probably the greatest cowboy of them all. Cooper's credibility on-screen owed much to the fact that he had in fact been a real-life cowboy before he got the acting bug and became an extra.

By 1927 he was starting a starring career which would thrill millions around the world, win him two acting Oscars (for *Sergeant York* in 1941 and the timeless *High Noon* in 1952) and a Special Academy Award in 1960 'for his many memorable screen performances and for the international recognition he, as an individual, has gained for the film industry.' For once, the Academy got it absolutely right.

MAY 1

Castro Abolishes Elections

Only two years after he and his guerrilla army swept to power in Cuba by deposing the corrupt regime of Fulgencio Batistá, and he had gone to great lengths to protest that he was not a communist, President Fidel Castro today showed his true colours by pronouncing Cuba a socialist nation.

El Presidente also announced that, as Cuba was now a socialist nation, it had no further need of democratic elections. They were abolished.

A Record 42-Year Sentence For Spy Blake

A PREVIOUSLY unmatched prison sentence of 42 years was passed on the former British diplomat, George Blake, in London's Old Bailey today after he had been convicted of spying for the Russians while working in positions which gave him almost unlimited access to many state secrets.

The 38-year-old, who had admitted to the charges, was believed to have been passing documents to Soviet contacts for almost ten years.

Blake had access to many types of top-secret and highly sensitive information while he was working in Germany and the Lebanon, and Lord Chief Justice Parker said that he had 'rendered much of this country's (Britain's) efforts completely useless' with his continued treachery.

The only mitigating aspect to Blake's actions seemed to be that he had been held for three years after being captured by the Communists during the Korean War, when he was Britain's vice-consul in the South Korean capital, Seoul. Held hostage, it was believed he may have been brainwashed by his captors.

Victorious Benn Banned Again

Four days after emerging victorious from the Bristol by-election called when his inheritance of a title made Labour MP Anthony Wedgwood Benn ineligible to sit as a Member of Parliament, the renegade politician was banned from the House of Commons today when he arrived to claim his seat.

Just before he, his family and a group of vocal supporters arrived at Westminster, the government had forced a vote to ensure that he would not be admitted to plead his case - a good one since he'd doubled his Bristol South-East majority.

It would take two years, and a change of law, before Mr Anthony Wedgwood Benn would be able to renounce his title, stand again for election, and return to the Commons as one of the most radical and articulate politicians of this century.

Anything U (SSR) Can Do...

Hot on the heels of Yuri Gagarin's pioneering manned space flight for the Soviet Space Agency, the United States' NASA responded today with an astronaut of its own - Commander Alan Shepard Jr of the US Navy, who flew to over 100 miles above the earth in a *Mercury* spacecraft.

During his flight, which lasted a quarter of an hour, Shepard was able to 'drive' his spaceship, something which Gagarin had not attempted. Like his Russian counterpart, Commander Shepard returned to earth uninjured, and in apparently perfect health.

Flushed with NASA's success, on May 25 President Kennedy predicted that the United States would be first to put a man on the moon.

MAY

JUNE 16

Russian Ballet Star In Airport Defection Drama

ONE OF THE MOST exciting new stars in the world of ballet, Russian dancer Rudolf Nureyev (pictured), was tonight in safe custody after staging a dramatic defection to the West at Le Bourget Airport, Paris, and making a successful plea for political asylum.

A leading member of Leningrad's Kirov Ballet, Nureyev was about to embark on a flight from Paris to London - where the Kirov was due to appear at Covent Garden - when he was approached in the customs hall by two Soviet officials and ordered to return to Moscow.

Nureyev, who dashed towards a group of gendarmes shouting 'Protect me! Protect me!', was later accompanied to talks at the Soviet Embassy by French police. Officials there were unable to change Nureyev's mind, and the 23-year-old began his new life under police protection.

JUNE 6

Psychologist Jung Dies At 85

Carl Gustav Jung, one of the giants of modern psychoanalysis, died today at the age of 85. Born in Switzerland, Jung worked for some time with Sigmund Freud, but broke away to found his own school. Jung attracted considerable interest in 1912 with his book, *The Theory Of Psychoanalysis*, and used thought-provoking and original classifications when considering the people he treated. Dubbing them either extrovert or introvert, he also classified them under four functions - feeling, thinking, sensation and intuition.

His basic philosophical difference with Freud related to the latter's concentration on sexual symbols, whereas Jung coined the term 'archetypes' for sub-personalities.

JUNE 19

Archaeologists Pinpoint Pilate

An Italian team of archaeologists working in Israel today uncovered evidence that Pontius Pilate definitely existed, nearly 2,000 years after his appearance in history.

The Roman governor, who is said to have tried Jesus Christ and ordered his crucifixion, was named - along with the Roman Emperor, Tiberius - on a large stone tablet excavated at Caesarea, near Haifa.

By strange coincidence, on the day after the find which proved the Bible historically accurate about Pilate, Nazi war criminal Adolf Eichmann - on trial in Jerusalem - agreed to give evidence, but refused to swear on the Bible!

JUNE 28

Court Declares Union Vote Invalid

A recent ballot held by Britain's Electrical Trades Union (ETU) was 'fixed' by its communist leadership, a London court decided today. The case, the first to be brought by members of a British union, effectively overturned the election of some of the ETU's executive and would force a fresh ballot to be held, with greater security for ballot papers and more independent counting procedures.

Only two months later, the ETU would be expelled from the Trades Union Congress for allowing vote rigging and, at the end of September, the TUC's National Executive Committee took similar action, isolating the electricians until democratic elections could be held.

UK TOP 10 SINGLES

1: Runaway
- Del Shannon
2: Surrender
- Elvis Presley
3: But I Do
- Clarence 'Frogman' Henry
4: Frightened City
- The Shadows
5: You'll Never Know
- Shirley Bassey
6: Hello Mary Lou/Travellin' Man
- Ricky Nelson
7: Halfway To Paradise
- Billy Fury
8: Have A Drink On Me
- Lonnie Donegan
9: Pasadena
- The Temperance Seven
10: More Than I Can Say
- Bobby Vee

JUNE 19

Iraq Claims Kuwait As UK Leaves

The first signs of a conflict which would finally explode into the 1991 Gulf War appeared this month as Britain - which had governed the tiny oil-rich kingdom of Kuwait as a protectorate since 1899 - handed control and full independence back on June 19.

Six days later, Kuwait's giant Arab neighbour, Iraq, declared that Kuwait was not independent, but was - and always had been - part of Iraq. The British had merely stolen it from Iraq, and now they wanted it back, along with its huge oil reserves and successful international banking system.

JUNE 27

Ramsey Created Archbishop Of Canterbury

In a solemn ceremony incorporating the 13th century marble throne of St Augustine, 56-year-old Dr Arthur Michael Ramsey was enthroned as the one hundredth Archbishop of Canterbury today.

The new head of the Church of England, who was Archbishop of York prior to this appointment, said that he hoped to make church services more accessible by allowing more flexibility in worship styles, and was clearly aware of the challenge facing him when talking of his task as the Anglican Church's 'chief shepherd'.

'It is a task beyond all human strength, and many are not so much hostile as indifferent and aloof,' he said. The climax of the ceremony was shown on television, the first time cameras had been allowed into Canterbury Cathedral.

JUNE 7

Britons Head For The Country

More and more Britons were quitting city and town centres to live in suburbs or beyond in the late 1950s, according to preliminary findings of the 1961 census published in London today - and Britain was getting more and more overcrowded.

Revealing that 52,675,094 people now occupied the British Isles - 2.5 million more than 10 years earlier - the census showed that an increased birth rate and a declining death rate had combined to boost the population, with 353,000 immigrants helping to create a situation which saw 790 people occupying each square mile of England and Wales.

Kennedy-Khrushchev Summit Fails To Reach Conclusions

PRESIDENT JOHN KENNEDY and his wife Jacqueline were greeted by huge cheering crowds when they arrived in London today for an overnight stay *en route* to America after Kennedy's inconclusive summit meeting with Russian leader Nikita Khrushchev in Vienna, the Austrian capital.

When the two met at Downing Street, the President explained to British Prime Minister Harold Macmillan that while no real progress had been made during his two days of meetings with Khrushchev, he felt that their talks may have helped lessen tension in Berlin, a city where the East-West divide had become most marked.

However, no progress was made on the reduction or banning of nuclear arsenals, but Kennedy noted that he had further clarified his country's intentions in several areas so that war would not result from any misunderstandings.

PLAYER PROVES HIS CLASS WITH US MASTERS WIN

Gary Player's victory in this year's US Masters at Augusta was memorable for a number of reasons. Not only did it mark the first time a foreigner had won the honour of donning the coveted champion's green jacket, but it was a victory won at the expense of reigning champion Arnold Palmer, a man apparently incapable of losing on US turf.

The win - which was the South African's second-only major title - also confirmed Player's astonishing consistency. Since winning the 1959 British Open he'd won no less than 25 other tournaments in Australia, Japan, South Africa, England, Egypt and the US, and managed 16 top-ten finishes on the PGA tour, half of which were in the top three.

Gary Player, aged 25 this year, had also overcome the real disability of lacking a long driving game in his early career. Only 5'7", he'd devised an exhausting and relentless physical fitness regime for himself, using weights and endurance routines to increase his natural strength.

Going into the Augusta clubhouse before Palmer, who drove off at the 18th a stroke ahead, Player and his wife Vivienne were forced to watch Arnie on TV. Despite an excellent first drive, Palmer got tangled in a bunker with his second shot.

Player had found himself in that same bunker earlier, but had managed to escape with a par. Palmer did not fare as well, and it took him five more shots to get down before he returned to the clubhouse to present Player with that green jacket.

BENFICA EMERGE TO WIN EUROPEAN CUP

The big football question this year was could the Spanish giants, Real Madrid, continue their dominance in the European Cup and win it for the sixth year in succession?

While experts suggested various teams who could end Real's fantastic run (mostly the big Italian clubs) in the final due to be played in Berne, all predictions turned out to be worthless when, to everyone's surprise and Real's horror, they were beaten by dreaded and deadly rivals Barcelona in the second round.

Spanish pride was salvaged by Barcelona continuing to that final, for a meeting with the Portuguese league champions, Benfica. Boasting most of Portugal's national team, Benfica were, however, pretty much an unknown quantity on the international stage, and were without the one player whose reputation had become established - the Mozambique-born striker, Eusebio.

They didn't need him, and Benfica emerged 3-2 winners to let the rest of Europe know that a new name would have to be included in all future prediction games.

HILL (PHIL, THAT IS) WINS WORLD MOTOR RACING CROWN

Ask any group of motor racing fans what the name Hill means to them, and the answer from the older ones would undoubtedly be 'Graham', while the younger would offer 'Damon'.

Fair enough. But there was another Hill good enough to become world champion. His name was Phil, and he was the first American to take the title when, as a member of Ferrari's all-conquering new team, his Belgian and Italian Grand Prix victories were enough to edge it for him.

Although Ferrari's new Tipo 156 also helped them win the constructors' championship, the season was marred by the death of their German driver, Ginther von Trips, in the Italian Grand Prix after he and Jim Clark collided.

Fourteen spectators also died in that incident, and Ferrari withdrew all of their team except for Hill. His victory at Monza secured him the title race, which von Trips had been leading narrowly before the race started.

Better known as a long-distance driver, Phil Hill - who was born in Miami, Florida, in 1929 - won the Le Man 24-hour Race in 1958 and 1961-62, the Sebring 12-hour in 1958, '59 and '61, and at Monza in 1960-61.

NOVEMBER 21:
ARRIVAL OF NADIA,
THE PERFECT GYMNAST

No one in the town of Onesti, in the Romanian region of Moldavia, could have known just how special today would prove to the world of gymnastics, and it would be six years before national athletics coaches realized what they had and began to train natural ability into perfect skill.

Nadia Comaneci was born today - the first gymnast in Olympic history to score a perfect 10.0, when her asymetric bars exercise in the 1976 Montreal Games proved flawless. She repeated her feat on the beam to help the Romanian women win a team silver medal before taking the individual golds - and five more tens - at both those exercises. In all, Nadia would win nine Olympic medals - five gold, three silver and a bronze - before ending her career at the 1981 World Student Games. A phenomenon whose bravery and ability took women's gymnastics to new heights, she defected from Romania in 1989 and settled in the US.

Nadia Comaneci

JULY 14

Space Ace Gagarin Flies In To Wow London

HAVING BEEN INTRODUCED yesterday to British Prime Minister Harold Macmillan - who called him 'a delightful fellow' - Russia's pioneering cosmonaut, Major Yuri Gagarin (pictured), was given an enthusiastic reception by huge crowds during a brief visit to London, which began officially today with lunch at Buckingham Palace with the Queen and the Duke of Edinburgh.

After a press conference at Earls Court, which was attended by an estimated 1,000 media representatives, the world's first spaceman flew (in an ordinary aircraft) to Manchester, where he was presented with a gold medal by the Amalgamated Union of Foundry Workers. A major public relations success by any standard, Gagarin's visit was considered above politics, even though commentators said it marked a new high in Anglo-Soviet relations. The British-Soviet Friendship Society called Gagarin 'a missile surely guided at the hearts of the British people'.

East Germans Flee To West

JULY 17

As fears increased that East Germany's Communist regime was about to cut links with West Germany and grab control of all access points to West Berlin, a massive flood of refugees was reported to be leaving the East, most of them headed for West Berlin. More than 1,800 were reported to have passed through West Berlin reception centres in the past 24 hours, many of them young families.

Algerian Rebels Sentenced To Death

Still hiding and on the run from police in Algeria and France, the leaders of the recent unsuccessful uprising in Algeria were all found guilty of treason in a Paris court today, and sentenced to death.

Among those whose sentences would have to wait until they were caught, was General Salan, the former French army commander whose opposition to Algerian independence led him to open revolt.

Tough Guy Writer Hemingway Found Dead

Celebrated American author Ernest Hemingway was found dead at his home in Idaho today, apparently killed by his own 12-bore shotgun.

Hemingway's fourth wife, Mary, who discovered the body of the 61-year-old novelist, issued a statement claiming the tough-guy writer - one of the most influential and successful writers of his generation - must have killed himself accidentally while cleaning his gun. He was wearing nightclothes when the tragedy occurred, and left no suicide note.

Ironically Hemingway's father, whose passion for hunting, shooting and fishing had been inherited by his son, had also shot and killed himself, an event which Ernest Hemingway had recalled in some of his literary work, which included the best-sellers *The Sun Also Rises*, *Death In The Afternoon* and T*he Old Man And The Sea*.

(See Came & Went pages for full appreciation)

US And USSR In Tit-For-Tat Defence Increases

Warning signs of an increased round of East-West sabre-rattling came this month when Soviet leader Nikita Khrushchev - who'd announced a major troop reduction plan at the end of last year - reversed his decision on July 9. Not only was he cancelling the cuts, he intended to increase military spending.

Warned by military chiefs that the US risked falling behind in arms development, President Kennedy called for increased defence spending on July 25. Good news for the American arms industry, but bad news for Washington doves looking for a more peaceful world.

UK TOP 10 SINGLES

1: Temptation
- The Everly Brothers
2: Runaway
- Del Shannon
3: Well I Ask You
- Eden Kane
4: Hello Mary Lou /Travellin' Man
- Ricky Nelson
5: A Girl Like You
- Cliff Richard
6: Pasadena
- The Temperance Seven
7: Halfway To Paradise
- Billy Fury
8: But I Do
- Clarence 'Frogman' Henry
9: Running Scared
- Roy Orbison
10: You Don't Know
- Helen Shapiro

JULY 31

Britain To Apply For Common Market Membership

BRITISH PRIME MINISTER Harold Macmillan today told a packed House of Commons that the UK intended to begin negotiations to join other European countries in the Common Market.

As Parliament erupted in a mixture of cheers and boos, Macmillan stressed that British membership would depend on suitable safeguards being in place to protect British farmers and trade with British Commonwealth nations, as well as the other members of EFTA - the European organization which Britain helped found with Sweden, Denmark, Norway, Portugal and Switzerland in 1959 as a rival to the Common Market.

The major stumbling block to Britain's application was envisaged as being the reaction of the French President, General de Gaulle, who was understood to oppose any special terms for Britain or the other EFTA members who were applying. Macmillan also faced strong opposition in Parliament, and he hinted that in the event of Britain's application being refused, there could be reductions in British contributions to NATO's defence budget.

JULY

Middleweight Champ Quits To Give Downes World Crown

The opportunity to cheer a British victory in a world championship fight had become almost as infrequent as the discovery of rocking-horse manure, but Paddington-born middleweight boxer Terry Downes achieved the almost impossible tonight at London's Wembley Arena when the defending American title-holder returned to his corner at the end of the ninth round and told his seconds he'd had enough.

Although the Boston-born champion, Paul Pender, appeared to have suffered far less facial damage than Downes, the cockney challenger had attacked hard during a fight which even seasoned veterans described as brutal. His relentless pummelling of Pender's body eventually forced the American to throw in the towel and hand Downes the crown.

Downes' victory came 10 years and a day after the unfancied Randolph Turpin won the same world title in London in similarly spectacular fashion by beating the legendary Sugar Ray Robinson.

All-British Wimbledon Final Shock

The increasingly rare occurrence of a British champion at the All-England tennis tournament at Wimbledon was greeted with partisan delight by a packed Centre Court today, all of whom were aware that it was 57 years since the Ladies Singles final had been an all-British

affair, so either Angela Mortimer or 20-year-old Christine Truman were guaranteed to register the first British win since 1937, when Dorothy Round won the championship.

The crowd favourite, Truman was tipped to take the crown, but it was an awkward fall by

her in the second set which proved the match's turning point. Limping, but gamely fighting on, she lost that set and was unable to stop Mortimer - a finalist in 1958 - winning a thrilling third set, and the crown. The score - 4-6,6-4,7-5.

35

West Rages As Berlin Wall Divides Germany

DESPITE A STORM of protest from Western leaders, the Communist authorities in East Germany acted to stem the flood of people escaping to the West this month by erecting a five feet high wall of concrete blocks to separate East Berlin from the US, British and French-controlled western half of the city.

Earlier in the month, the border between the two sectors of Berlin had been blocked by barbed wire barricades and, despite a plea for calm from the Mayor of Berlin, Willi Brandt, and demands by America, Britain and France for the Russian-backed regime of Walter Ulbricht to desist from 'illegal restrictions', the East German government built the wall to make the barrier permanent.

As each day passed, the wall was reinforced and strengthened from the Eastern side, and by the end of the month, it had become clear that no amount of protest from the Western powers would stop the communists reinforcing it, despite the positioning of tanks and 1,000 troops along the western side of the wall.

A particularly disturbing escalation of the Cold War between the USA and the USSR, the wall was described by American Secretary of State Dean Rusk as 'a flagrant violation of the right of free circulation throughout the city in direct contravention of the Four Power agreement', which was signed in 1949 by Russia, the US, Britain and France.

The appearance of the wall caused serious unrest on both sides of the city. While West Berliners staged protests, many in the East made it clear that they had no desire to be effectively imprisoned and so unable to visit relatives and friends in the West. As East German engineers began clearing strips of wooded country on Berlin's outskirts, refugees were reported to be finding new ways of escaping to the West.

AUGUST 10

Teenager Helen Tops UK Charts

Helen Shapiro, a 14-year-old London schoolgirl whose distinctive deep voice helped bring her immediate fame, today topped the British pop chart with her second single, *You Don't Know*.

The record was reported to have sold 40,000 copies in a single day, knocking Eden Kane's *Well I Ask You* off the top spot. Pundits rightly predicted that *You Don't Know* would become an equally big hit in many other parts of the world.

Helen was discovered by record producer John Schroeder, who met her by chance when she was attending her weekly singing lesson in London's West End. Schroeder not only produced her hits, but also wrote them.

AUGUST 7

Russian Cosmonaut Stays Aloft For A Whole Day

A second Russian spaceman, 26-year-old Major Gherman Titov, created a new endurance record for space travel today when he orbited the earth 17 times during a 25-hour flight.

Russian television transmitted pictures of Major Titov eating meals and sleeping in his *Vostok* spacecraft. There had been concern about the effects of prolonged exposure to conditions outside the earth's atmosphere on human beings, but Titov was pronounced in perfect health on his return from his epic voyage.

AUGUST 30

Miraculous Escape In The Mountains

One of the most incredible and terrifying ordeals imaginable ended triumphantly today when 63 tourists were rescued from a stranded cable car in France. Although there were six fatalities in the incident, officials described the rescue of survivors as 'nothing short of a miracle'.

The disaster occurred when a low-flying jet cut through the cable from which the car was suspended, hundreds of feet above the ground.

AUGUST 21

Kenyatta Allowed Freedom Of Movement

THE NATIONALIST leader of Kenya, Jomo Kenyatta, was today freed from eight years in custody by his British captors, and told he could join other African leaders at a London conference to settle his country's future independence.

Found guilty in 1953 of involvement in the terrorist Mau Mau organization, Kenyatta's dominance in the Kenyan nationalist movement was only confirmed by the repeated refusal of other Kenyan leaders to discuss or support British attempts to introduce political reforms while he remained in prison.

In 1959, Kenyatta was moved from a remote prison camp to a house on the outskirts of Nairobi, but his movements had remained restricted until the British District Commissioner visited the 71-year-old to tell him that he was no longer detained.

Commentators were unanimously predicting that Kenyatta would become Kenya's first leader once the country won its independence, so following the likes of Archbishop Makarios of Cyprus as a president who'd survived British capture, exile or imprisonment before emerging as a national leader.

AUGUST 16

London's PO Tower Gains 96 Feet

Civil engineers employed in the construction of London's newest landmark building, the GPO Tower, today confirmed that it would be taller than originally planned - 603 ft, and not 507 ft.

The tower, which will be Britain's tallest building when completed, will be topped by a mass of communications equipment. That, and the inclusion of a revolving restaurant and a public observation centre, appear to have made the Post Office's showcase a lot bigger than expected.

AUGUST 14

Eichmann Trial Ends

The five month trial of former SS chief Adolf Eichmann, accused of materminding the Nazi's 'final solution' extermination of millions of Jews, gypsies and dissidents during WWII, ended in Jerusalem today.

While Eichmann's admission of guilt on a number of conspiracy charges meant he faced the death penalty, a world wide clemency appeal had been launched, with the Israeli judicial panel being asked not to order Eichmann hanged. While no one excused Eichmann, or his part in the Holocaust, many believed that Israel could provide a moral lead by showing mercy.

MPs Agree British Common Market Application

AUGUST 4

The British government today got the official go-ahead it needed to authorize its decision to apply for membership of the Common Market when, despite Labour opposition to the move, the House of Commons voted for the application to be made.

Prime Minister Harold Macmillan knew only too well that this would be only the first of many future hurdles Britain would have to face.

With a number of his own party against Market membership, a large percentage of the British population said to be against the application, and General de Gaulle known to be wary of British inclusion in the 'club' dominated by France and Germany, Macmillan prepared for a long and rocky road when Britain's application was formally lodged on August 10.

Helen Delivers Britain's Answer To Brenda

Given the breakthrough of US teenager Brenda Lee in 1960, it was only a matter of time before British talent scouts came up with a local girl to hit the market which obviously existed for a precocious, big-voiced adolescent. The arrival of Helen Shapiro was not unexpected, then. But her astonishing abilities and maturity were.

The discovery of EMI's top producer Norrie Paramor and songwriter John Schroeder, Helen would burst onto the British scene in March with the aptly titled *Don't Treat Me Like A Child*, and immediately create a rush by journalists to the Bethnal Green register of births and deaths to confirm that this astonishingly mature voice did belong to a 14-year-old.

By year-end, Helen would release two further singles - *You Don't Know* and *Walkin' Back To Happiness* - and score No 1 hits with both to confirm she was no novelty act, something early detractors had suggested. In 1962, she scored four more big hits with *Tell Me What He Said, Let's Talk About Love, Little Miss Lonely* and *Keep Away From Other Girls*, starred in the musical movie *It's Trad, Dad* and started the move into cabaret to ensure that, when the Beatles-led group boom shoved many 'old-fashioned' performers into oblivion, she still had a very active and successful career.

With many ups and downs, that career moved through a period in stage musicals to arrive at a well-deserved reputation as an accomplished jazz singer with an engagement diary constantly full for a couple of years ahead.

BEN E GOES SOLO TO CREATE CLASSICS

Singers who leave successful groups to go solo invariably find themselves sidelined, their best moments remaining the work they did as a team member. If you immediately thought 'What about Diana Ross and The Supremes, Michael Jackson and The Jackson Five, Brian Ferry and Roxy Music, or Peter Gabriel and Genesis?' you've probably come up with the few exceptions which prove the rule.

So Ben E King's descision to leave the US hit machine called The Drifters early this year raised quite a few eyebrows, not least because King (real name Benjamin Arnold) was so much the voice of that group, no one could see how they'd continue without him, and how he'd cope without their wonderful support.

As it happened, The Drifters would replace King with the soundalike Rudy Lewis and start a run of huge international hits to equal the King-led smashes *Dance With Me, Save The Last Dance For Me* and *I Count The Tears* - among them *When My Little Girl Is Smiling, Under The Boardwalk* and *Come On Over To My Place*.

As for Mr King, he'd start his solo career with two absolute classics which would guarantee him immortality - the Phil Spector/Jerry Leiber composed *Spanish Harlem* and *Stand By Me*, a song King wrote with Leiber and Leiber's long-time partner, Mike Stoller.

Through the next seven years King would string together a dozen or more US hits before switching direction to concentrate mostly on performing live. In 1986 *Stand By Me* would re-emerge as the title and theme song for a hugely-successful movie, and become an international No 1 all over again.

BILLY FURY - THE UNSUNG HERO

It's strange how time has been so unfair to Billy Fury, who - along with Cliff Richard, Marty Wilde and Adam Faith - ruled the British rock and pop scene in the late 1950s and early 1960s with an unbroken run of huge hits, but is invariably overlooked by music historians.

Born Ronald Wycherly in Liverpool, Fury was given his new name by British rock impresario Larry Parnes in 1958 and began his hit-making early in 1959 with the moody *Maybe Tomorrow*. There were three more hits in 1960, but it was this year which saw Fury's star ascend to really great heights with *A Thousand Stars* (his version of the Kathy Young US hit), *Don't Worry, Halfway To Paradise, I'll Never Find Another You* and *Jealousy*.

While all of his most successful records - he had more than twenty British Top 20 hits among his thirty-plus chart entries between 1959 and his death from a heart attack in 1983 - were often dramatic ballads, Fury recorded at least one hard-core rockabilly album, *The Sound Of Fury*, to prove that he could have just as easily made it as Britain's most authentic rock 'n' roll artist.

Helen Shapiro

SEPT

CND Demo - 850 Arrested

EIGHT HUNDRED AND FIFTY ban-the-bomb demonstrators were arrested today as more than 15,000 Campaign For Nuclear Disarmament (CND) supporters - the biggest rally staged in London to date -packed Trafalgar Square to demand the end of nuclear weapons.

Among those arrested and later charged with breaches of the peace or obstructing police, were the CND Chairman, Canon John Collins, as well as several celebrity supporters, including actress Vanessa Redgrave, playwright John Osborne and George Melly, the noted jazz singer.

Violence erupted when some of the 3,000 police in attendance tried to move people who were sitting on pavements and refusing to budge, after which the arrests began.

Fittingly, the rally coincided with the test explosion of a bomb by the Russians. It followed the prison sentences imposed, only days before, on two other high profile protesters - the noted philosopher Bertrand Russell and John Osborne's fellow playwright, Arnold Wesker.

De Gaulle Survives Assassination Bid

One of the French generals responsible for organizing the abortive rebellion in Algeria, Raoul Salan, was today accused of attempting to assassinate the French President, Charles de Gaulle.

A plastic explosive charge had been fired at the President's car by members of an organization known as The Secret Army, near his country home of Colombey-les-Deux-Eglises. The President's personal security staff had arrested one of the perpetrators, who had identified his colleagues in the plot and named its major architect as ex-General Salan.

An apparently calm de Gaulle called the attempt on his life 'a joke in very bad taste'.

SEPTEMBER 13

Spectators Killed In Monza Death Crash

The real risks of motor racing were made horribly clear at the Monza race track today when 13 Italian Grand Prix spectators were killed in a crash which also claimed the life of German driver Wolfgang von Trips.

The tragedy occurred when the German's Ferrari collided with British driver Jim Clark's Lotus and von Trips' machine somersaulted into spectators watching from nearby grass verges.

The re-started race was won by Britain's Graham Hill, a victory which gave him the 1961 World Championship. Sadly, von Trips had been leading the title race when he died, having scored two wins and a second place.

UK TOP 10 SINGLES

UK TOP 10 SINGLES

1: Johnny Remember Me
- John Leyton
2: You Don't Know
- Helen Shapiro
3: Reach For The Stars/Climb Ev'ry Mountain
- Shirley Bassey
4: Wild In The Country
- Elvis Presley
5: Kon-Tiki
- The Shadows
6: Cupid
- Sam Cooke
7: Well I Ask You
- Eden Kane
8: Michael Row The Boat
- The Highwaymen
9: That's My Home
- Acker Bilk
10: Romeo
- Petula Clark

SEPTEMBER 23

A New Star In New York?

There was great excitement in New York folk music circles this month at the arrival of a new and promising performer from Minnesota named Bob Dylan, who wrote thought-provoking songs and began a week as headline attraction at the Greenwich Village club, Gerde's Folk City, tonight.

The 20-year-old came to New York to visit his idol, left-wing songwriter Woody Guthrie, who was in hospital suffering from a rare disease known as Huntington's Chorea. There was a feeling that Dylan's style owed much to Guthrie's influence. The new kid in town had just been signed to Columbia Records by John Hammond, who also discovered the great blues singer, Bessie Smith.

Hammond encountered Dylan during the production of an album by Carolyn Hester, a Texan singer who was friendly with the late Buddy Holly. Hester invited Dylan to play harmonica on her record, and Hammond, impressed by the youngster's talent, made him an offer he couldn't refuse.

SEPTEMBER 14

Mothercare Opens For Business

A new and welcome arrival to British shopping centres opened its doors for the first time today, heralding the start of what would prove one of the great success stories of the next three decades.

Mothercare, a shop dedicated entirely to merchandise for mothers-to-be, new mothers and their children, opened for business in the South London suburb of Kingston-upon-Thames.

UN's Hammarskjöld Killed In Mystery Air Crash

DÄG HAMMARSKJÖLD, the United Nations' dynamic Secretary-General, paid the ultimate price for his hands-on approach to peace-keeping today when he was killed in a plane crash *en route* for talks aimed at ending the Congo civil war. The DC6 airliner in which he was travelling to Northern Rhodesia suddenly dropped out of the sky after an explosion, which many blamed on sabotage.

The 56-year-old Hammarskjöld was on his way to Ndola for a meeting with the Katangan leader, Moise Tshombe, who'd taken refuge in Northern Rhodesia after United Nations forces had suppressed attempts by his Katangan rebels to separate the province from the newly-independent republic of Congo.

While UN forces from India and Hammarskjöld's native country of Sweden had succeeded in stamping out the rebellion on September 13, many questioned whether UN representative Dr Conor Cruise O'Brien had been justified in ordering the action, in which almost 100 were said to have died.

The only survivor of the crash reported that just as the aircraft had been about to land at Ndola, Mr Hammarskjöld had instructed the pilot to remain airborne. Shortly after there had been an explosion.

At an emergency session of the UN's Security Council in New York, the Soviet delegate publicly dissociated his government from a communiqué praising Hammarskjöld's diplomatic skills and leadership. On October 23 the rest of the world's true feelings were reflected in the Nobel Awards committee announcement that Däg Hammarskjöld's services would be recognized by a posthumous Nobel Peace Prize.

Syria Quits United Arab Republic

Syria declared its independence from the United Arab Republic today, only two days after troops in Damascus staged a revolt against Egyptian domination of the alliance formed by the the late President Nasser in the mid-1950s.

It was Nasser's dream to form a coalition of Arab states which could act together against Western imperialism and create a common front against Israel. That dream would seem to be in tatters as Syrians showed their resentment against Egyptian superiority and enforced nationalization of local industries, and the deportation of 25,000 Egyptian nationals was ordered.

Turkish Ex-Premier Hanged

Adnan Menderes, the former Turkish Prime Minister who helped conclude the agreement which settled terms for the independence of Cyprus in 1959, was hanged today in a prison on Imrali island where he'd been held since being found guilty of breaking his country's constitution.

Forced by runaway inflation and widespread unrest to suspend the constitution in April last year, the 62-year-old Menderes was overthrown by a military coup only a month later.

OCTOBER 20

Algerian Women Take Their Fight To France

THE CONTINUING CIVIL war for independence in Algeria reached the streets of Paris and other northern French cities today as thousands of Muslim women staged passive demonstrations against a curfew introduced by President de Gaulle to counter the growing threat of terrorism in France.

The women staged the protest marches while their husbands and other men were on strike. They were organized by the National Liberation Front (FLN) to prove that the large number of Algerian expatriates were under their control.

Despite the non-violent stance taken by the women, some of whom carried babies, they were met by armed riot police. In Nanterre, a centre for FLN activities, more than 1,000 of the women and children were put on buses and taken into custody pending identity checks.

In Algeria itself, on October 31, marches staged to mark the seventh anniversary of the 1954 Muslim rebellion went off less peaceably. Eighty-six people died in riots which broke out when police attempted to halt events.

OCTOBER 11

You Wanna Da Bad Noos? Chico Died

Chico Marx, the brother who tortured the English language to such an extent that it often took Groucho half a page of fast-fire gags to discover what he'd meant to say when he first said what he wanted to say, and played the piano with such abandoned brilliance, died today. He was 75 years old.

With the eccentric logic which attached itself to everything the Marx Brothers did, Leonard Marx transformed himself into the barely intelligible Italian stooge Chico, while Adolph stopped talking altogether and - because he played the harp beautifully - became Harpo. Younger brother Julius became the cigar-chomping, wise-cracking, wimmin-chasing Groucho.

Born in New York and pushed into a vaudeville career by a dominating mother, the Marx Brothers (five originally, but two went into other things) became stars on Broadway before Hollywood beckoned in 1929 and they began making some of the funniest, strangest and most timeless comedy films ever. When they stopped making films in 1950, Chico and Harpo called it quits and retired, while Groucho went into television and legend.

Augustus John, Gypsy Painter, Dies

The European art world lost a flamboyant character and a fine portrait painter today, with the death of Augustus John. He was 83, a remarkable age for a larger-than-life man whose amorous and pleasure-filled lifestyle was legendary.

Born in Wales, John spent much of his childhood travelling in a caravan with his Bohemian parents. He would seek out the company of gypsies in his later life, both for their companionship and their inspiration for his work.

His portraits of such leading figures as Dylan Thomas, TE Lawrence, Thomas Hardy, George Bernard Shaw and WB Yeats gained him acclaim and fame, though John himself always said that his sister Gwen, who died in 1939, was the real painter of the family.

JANUARY 10
DASHIELL HAMMETT - THE SILENT REVOLUTIONARY

The man who created the fast-talking, quick-thinking private detective Sam Spade, US author Dashiell Hammett - who died today at the age of 67 - lived an eventful life packed with every bit as much excitement and incident as any of the fictional ones which helped make his name.

Hammett's early experiences as a real-life detective with the legendary Pinkerton Agency became the inspiration for the short stories which encouraged him to become a full-time writer. His ability to create vivid word pictures inevitably led to Hollywood recognizing the potential of his thrillers, two of which - *The Maltese Falcon* and *The Thin Man* - became classics.

Not only did the latter spawn five big-screen sequels, but it would provide Peter Lawford with regular employment in a TV series in the late 1950s. And while Humphrey Bogart's definitive Sam Spade made the 1941 version of *The Maltese Falcon* the classic version, it was also filmed under that title in 1931, as *Satan Met A Lady* in 1936, and was spoofed by director John Huston (who made the Bogart version) in 1954 as *Beat The Devil*.

A fervent socialist, Hammett was imprisoned in 1951 when he refused to tell the Un-American Activities Committee witch-hunters the source of funds he was administering for a political group they alleged was a Communist Party front. He never wrote again, settling for a relatively quiet life with his long-time companion, the writer Lillian Hellman.

JULY 2
ERNEST HEMINGWAY - THE MACHO MAESTRO

No one wrote like Ernest Hemingway, the Nobel Prize-winning novelist who shot himself today, unable - and unwilling - to cope with the long illness which dogged his last years and left him unable to carry on the macho lifestyle he mirrored so vividly in books like *The Sun Also Rises, A Farewell To Arms, Death In The Afternoon* and *For Whom The Bell Tolls* during the 1920s and 1930s.

Born in 1899, in Illinois, Hemingway began his life-long passion for fishing and hunting at an early age. After serving with an ambulance unit during World War I he settled in Paris in a literary exile community which included Gertrude Stein and Ezra Pound.

A war correspondent during the Spanish Civil War and World War II, his experiences in the former helped inspire the writing of *For Whom The Bell Tolls* in 1940, but it was the revival of his skills evidenced by his novella *The Old Man And The Sea* in 1952 which encouraged the Nobel committee to award him the 1954 Literature Prize.

Ernest Hemingway fishing in Cuba

DECEMBER 12
DANIEL O'DONNELL - IRELAND'S COUNTRY SUPERSTAR

It's a measure of the outstanding success enjoyed by Irish country music singer Daniel O'Donnell, who was born today in Kincasslagh, County Donegal, that Britain's major record companies tried, in 1991, to have his records disqualified from the British country charts.

They said it was because his albums weren't country at all, but middle-of-the-road pop. In reality, British country fans were buying so many Daniel O'Donnell records, new releases by supposedly 'major' US stars weren't selling enough in comparison to win inclusion in a chart featuring as many as five O'Donnell albums!

The youngest brother of the 1970s country star known simply as Margo, O'Donnell learned his stage skills as a backing singer in her band and, after recording a few reasonably successful singles, signed with the independent Irish label, Ritz Records. With them, O'Donnell went on to develop an international career which has included a string of best-selling albums and in-concert videos, sell-out appearances in the biggest concert halls of Britain, the US and Australia, and recording in Nashville with Allen Reynolds, the producer responsible for the biggest hits of US country. Six of his albums have entered the country charts at No 1, while one of his videos - *An Evening With Daniel O'Donnell* - spent a remarkable 18 months in the British Music Video chart.

That 1991 chart disqualification was short-lived, by the way. Outraged fans - including one very angry nun - raised such a storm, that young Daniel's right to inclusion was won back after only two months. The first chart published after his return featured six of his albums!

NOV

Kennedy Orders More US 'Advisers' For Vietnam

THE ESCALATING conflict in Vietnam, where the North Vietnamese communist regime of Ho Chi Minh had been mounting increasingly effective attacks on South Vietnam's forces, moved closer to outright war today with President Kennedy's announcement of further military aid to the South.

During the next two years, the number of US military 'advisers' available to South Vietnam was to be increased to 16,000, the President said, with the immediate addition of an extra 200 US Air Force instructors joining the 700 US army staff already in place.

An airfield had been prepared and equipped to the north-east of South Vietnam's capital, Saigon, in readiness for the imminent arrival of US bombers. Further support in the shape of helicopters, fighter planes, radar equipment and road vehicles, was to follow soon.

Britain Sets Limits On Immigrants

The British government tonight acted to curb the rising number of Commonwealth immigrants arriving in Britain and claiming residential rights. The move followed publication of data which showed that while just over 20,000 had settled in the UK in 1959, up to 100,000 were expected to have done likewise in 1961.

In future, a new qualification system would apply - only those who had a job to come to, who could support themselves, or had skills which would enable them to find work, would be able to apply for a voucher granting them the right to live in Britain. But the scheme came under attack from Labour Party leader Hugh Gaitskell when it was revealed that there would be an annual limit on the number of vouchers issued. They were to be allocated strictly on a 'first come, first served' basis. It was, said Mr Gaitskell, immigration control on an unacceptable level.

Thurber's Dogs Wail No More

American author, humourist and cartoonist James Thurber died today at the age of 66.

Widely known throughout the world for his quirky and often surreal cartoons in which droopy dogs played a constant role, Thurber also created an abiding legend in his short story *The Secret Life Of Walter Mitty,* which became an international hit for comedian Danny Kaye when filmed in 1947.

A regular contributor to *The New Yorker* magazine, Thurber also wrote a number of fantasies for children, a species to which he consistently claimed membership.

Queen Ignores Ghanaian Bomb Threats

The state visit to Ghana of HRH Queen Elizabeth and the Duke of Edinburgh began as planned today, despite rumours of bomb plots from rebel elements in the West African country.

Ghana achieved independence in 1957, when its name was changed from the Gold Coast, its release from colonial status reflecting the 'wind of change' which British Prime Minister Harold Macmillan predicted was affecting much of the continent. The royal visit had been scheduled for 1960, but the birth of Prince Andrew had forced a postponement.

At an official banquet tonight, President Nkrumah assured the Queen that no matter what happened in the rest of Africa, he and the Ghanaian people would still hold her and her husband in great regard. In her reply, the Queen complimented Ghana on its 'energy and sense of purpose'.

UK TOP 10 SINGLES

1: His Latest Flame
- Elvis Presley
2: Walkin' Back To Happiness
- Helen Shapiro
3: Take Good Care Of My Baby
- Bobby Vee
4: Big Bad John
- Jimmy Dean
5: When The Girl In Your Arms Is The Girl In Your Heart
- Cliff Richard
6: Take Five
- The Dave Brubeck Quartet
7: Hit The Road Jack
- Ray Charles
8: The Time Has Come
- Adam Faith
9: Sucu-Sucu
- Laurie Johnson
10: Mexicali Rose
- Karl Denver

NOVEMBER 11

Stalinists Expelled From Soviet Communist Party

The purge of former Soviet dictator Josef Stalin's reputation which led to his body being exhumed and removed from its place of honour in the Kremlin last month, gained pace today when the all-powerful Communist Party turned on a number of men who'd once actively supported his views and brutal methods.

Such internationally known figures as former Prime Minister Georgi Malenkov and ex-Foreign Minister Vyacheslav Molotov were among those expelled from the Party, effectively a death sentence as far as their public lives and future career prospects were concerned.

In the meantime, Stalin's fall continued with the destruction of every memorial and statue in the Soviet Union, and a re-titling of every street, square and public venue bearing his name.

NOVEMBER 3

Burma's U Thant Appointed To UN Hot-Seat

BURMESE DIPLOMAT U Thant was today unanimously chosen to follow Däg Hammarskjöld as the United Nations Secretary-General, pitching him into the heart of the continuing Congolese civil war and a number of disturbing new developments.

The first crisis confronting the 52-year-old came with reports that Katangan leader Moise Tshombe had violated the ceasefire negotiated by his predecessor, when he launched an air strike on Congolese government troops.

In his turn, Tshombe accused the UN of helping ferry Congolese troops to the Katangan border, so breaking its neutrality. The Katangan president's view of the UN would not be improved on October 14 when an official report into the death of Congo ex-premier Patrice Lumumba in January accused Tshombe and Congo President Kasavubu of conspiring his murder.

Most bizarrely - and horribly - on September 14 U Thant was forced to order the arrest and punishment of those who sold the bodies of 13 Italian UN troops in a Congo market.

NOVEMBER 19

Tank Traps Boost Berlin Wall

Determined to continue developing the Berlin Wall despite continued West Berlin demonstrations and the condemnation of Western governments, the East German regime acted decisively against the threat of invasion from the West today when work began on the installation of tank traps.

They were to be positioned in the no-man's land the East Germans had created by tearing down huge tracts of forest and demolishing almost all buildings near the border.

Don And Phil Join The Marines

Top American pop star brothers Don and Phil Everly answered Uncle Sam's call today and were inducted into the US Marine Corps for an initial six months of active service.

Shorn of their locks, the makers of such hits as *When Will I Be Loved, Cathy's Clown, Dream* and *Wake Up Little Susie* would spend some of their service spell performing on top-rated TV shows in full uniform. Unlike Elvis Presley, who opted to become a normal unpublic soldier, The Everly Brothers won an early release from duty by becoming one of the Marine Corps' most active marketing ploys.

NOV

Eichmann Sentenced To Death

NAZI WAR CRIMINAL Adolf Eichmann was sentenced to be hanged by a court in Jerusalem today after being declared guilty of the murder of millions of Jewish people during World War II.

Eichmann - who had been brought to Jerusalem to face 15 charges of mass murder and complicity after being captured by Israeli secret service agents in Argentina - showed no emotion as Mr Justice Landau pronounced: 'This court sentences the accused to death for crimes against the Jewish people, crimes against humanity, and war crimes.'

The sentencing, more or less a formality after Eichmann admitted conspiracy in Hitler's 'final solution', was in anti-climactic contrast to the often harrowing drama of the trial itself. As the court rose, Eichmann turned on his heels and left the bullet proof glass box which had been built to protect him from potential assassins. He would be hanged on May 31, 1962.

Eichmann's capture and arrest in Argentina, where he'd been living under an assumed name ever since disappearing at the end of the war in May, 1945, confirmed well-founded suspicions that many erstwhile members of Hitler's Nazi organization had fled to South America when their leader died. A large number were believed to still be in Argentina, where several groups of neo-Nazi sympathizers were known to exist.

Music History Made As Marvelettes Become First Motown Chart-Toppers

The shape and direction of American popular music changed forever today when Motown, the black-controlled independent record company based in Detroit, Michigan, achieved what would prove to be only the first of many records to top the US singles chart published by *Billboard,* the music trade magazine.

For the record, the historical disc was *Please Mr Postman* by The Marvelettes. The song would later be recorded by The Beatles, and be a 1970s hit for The Carpenters.

Motown Records was founded

and owned by Berry Gordy Jr, an ex-professional boxer who had enjoyed some success as a songwriter in the late 1950s when vocalist Jackie Wilson recorded several of his songs. Convinced that he had never received the financial rewards he believed were due to him, Gordy decided to launch his own label.

Among the artists he would discover, sign and steer to stardom, would be Diana Ross and The Supremes, Smokey Robinson, Marvin Gaye, The Four Tops, Stevie Wonder and Michael Jackson.

Birth Pill Available Via NHS

Controversy arose in Britain today as church groups combined with conservative parents and some elements of the medical profession to protest at the government's decision to make birth control pills available on the National Health Service.

Opponents argued that the Pill's greater availability would lead to an increase in under-age sex, to teenagers taking it without their parents' permission, and an inevitable growth in cases of sexually transmitted diseases.

UK TOP 10 SINGLES

1: Tower Of Strength
- Frankie Vaughan
2: Moon River
- Danny Williams
3: Take Good Care Of My Baby
- Bobby Vee
4: Midnight In Moscow
- Kenny Ball's Jazzmen
5: Stranger On The Shore
- Mr Acker Bilk
6: I'll Get By
- Shirley Bassey
7: Walkin' Back To Happiness
- Helen Shapiro
8: His Latest Flame
- Elvis Presley
9: Johnny Will
- Pat Boone
10: Take Five
- The Dave Brubeck Quartet

Indians Win Back Goa

Four hundred years of Portuguese control of Goa, the enclave located on the western side of the Indian sub-continent, ended today when Indian forces over-ran the territory, forcing the Governor, General Silva,

to surrender.

The determination of India to recapture the province made the battle one-sided, as Indian paratroops and warships poured into what turned out to be a very brief

fight. In one episode of bravery, a Portuguese frigate, *Alfonso de Albuquerque,* went into battle with three Indian warships. She was smashed with gunfire before being beached by her wounded captain.

DECEMBER 1

UN Fires Irish Diplomat From Congo Post

DR CONOR CRUISE O'BRIEN (pictured), the Irish diplomat who apparently defied the neutral standing of the United Nations in the Congo civil war in September when he ordered UN troops to suppress Katanga's attempt to go it alone, was 'relieved' of his post today.

A United Nations official announced that Dr O'Brien had been 'released' at the request of the Irish government, although his departure came as little surprise. While the Western powers had been critical of what was seen as his undemocratic solution to the Katangan situation, he was popular with many Asian and African countries, who felt he had acted correctly. One of his most prominent supporters, Ghanaian President Kwame Nkrumah, personally offered his best wishes.

Dr O'Brien, who was about to marry another Irish UN representative, Maire MacEntee, apparently felt that he had been victimized by the British government. It had, he said, maintained pressure for his sacking when the immediate controversy had died down.

DECEMBER 21

Tshombe Abandons Dreams Of Independence

The conflict in the Congo officially ended today when Katangan President Moise Tshombe finally admitted defeat in the three-month power struggle over Katanga's unilateral declaration of independence from the newly-independent Congo.

While the United Nations' involvement in the dispute was sometimes worthy of criticism, its intervention ultimately convinced Tshombe to accept the fact that Katanga had acted wrongly in attempting to secede, and would have to revert to its status as one of six Congolese provinces.

Signing a statement acknowledging that fact, and handing control of Katangan armed forces to Congolese Prime Minister Cyrille Adoula, Mr Tshombe conceded defeat after uninterrupted talks lasting more than 18 hours.

Decimalization For Britain?

The British government today decided that, at some point in the future, it may consider the prospect of decimalization of coinage, weights and measures to bring Britain into line with most, if not all, of the rest of the world.

Such a move would also end the confusion felt by foreign visitors who found it difficult to grasp such concepts as 240 pence to £1, eight pints to a gallon or 16 ounces to 1lb.

The government was under no illusion that decimalization would be easily introduced. Traditionalists had already made it clear that they'd fight change all the way.

Take Me To Cuba!

A new, disturbing and ultimately counter-productive form of international terrorism emerged for the first time today when Cuban hijackers forced a US airliner captain to fly his craft and passengers to Havana and a hero's welcome for his armed captors.

The following months would see a spate of copy-cat hijacks, a massive increase of security at world airports, and a new source of material for comedians.

Unlike most Western horoscope systems which group astrological signs into month-long periods based on the influence of 12 constellations, the Chinese believe that those born in the same year of their calendar share common qualities, traits and weaknesses with one of 12 animals - Rat, Ox, Tiger, Rabbit, Dragon, Snake, Horse, Sheep, Monkey, Rooster, Dog or Pig.

They also allocate the general attributes of five natural elements - Earth, Fire, Metal, Water, Wood - and an overall positive or negative aspect to each sign to summarize its qualities.

If you were born between January 28, 1950 and February 14, 1961, you are a Rat. As this book is devoted to the events of 1961, let's take a look at the sign which governs those born between February 15 that year and February 4, 1962 - The Year of The Ox

THE OX
FEBRUARY 15, 1961 - FEBRUARY 4, 1962
ELEMENT: METAL   ASPECT: (-)

Oxen individuals are solid, even stolid characters with strong personalities. Trustworthy and dependable, they seek integrity and always face their responsibilities. They are kind, caring souls, full of common sense and very down to earth. Very preoccupied with security, they are ready to work long and hard to provide a nest for themselves.

Despite this need for security, Oxen are also strong-minded, individualistic - and don't take kindly to being told what to do. They are, in fact, quite dominant and have high standards of excellence, like to make rules and tend to dislike those who step out of line. They have to learn to be more tolerant of those around them if they want to live in a peaceful environment.

Oxen are quiet, steady and methodical, preferring to be in the background rather than be pushed to the front. However, they can display leadership qualities when necessary, adopting a commanding presence and an ability to take charge. They easily earn the respect and loyalty of others.

Even though they don't like to be in the limelight, the Oxen's strong-minded willpower and conscientious attitude will see them to the top, sooner or later. Practical, conservative and traditional, they believe in building things bit by bit, and always based on solid ground. They can be very stylish and individualistic in the way they look, and know how to present themselves.

Oxen are very affectionate to those close to their hearts, but quite cool and distant with strangers. Once Oxen commit themselves, they're loyal, deep and passionate, even if they seem to lack originality and romance. But they also have a tendency to retreat into themselves when they suffer, and don't cry out their emotions.

Oxen are conservative in many aspects of life, but for them conservatism goes with emotion and commitment. They like to build solid, secure foundations in life and plan everything carefully. Hard work, tenacity and loyalty take them to the top, where Oxen enjoy being quietly dominant.

FAMOUS OXEN

HRH The Princess of Wales

HRH Viscount Linley
eldest son of Princess Margaret

Richard Nixon
former President of the United States

Margaret Thatcher
former Prime Minister of Britain

Gerald Ford
former Vice President of the United States

Jane Fonda
Oscar-winning actress, former political activist

Robert Redford
Oscar-winning actor, director, conservationist

Dustin Hoffman
Oscar-winning actor, noted perfectionist